W9-AJQ-747

# Table of Contents

# Introduction

Wherever she is, whether at home or at work, Mrs. Murphy regularly experiences her husband's now famous Murphy's Law: If anything can go wrong, it will. At the prompting of her good friend, Mrs. Webster of **Mrs. Webster's Dictionary**, Mrs. Murphy decided to write her own laws–those relating to the daily lives of women. She hopes you enjoy reading it as much as she enjoyed writing it.

She would also like to dedicate this book to Larry, who bravely suggested she write it, and to the memory of Roy V. Selstad.

# Mrs. Murphy's Laws

Great Quotations Publishing Company
Glendale Heights, Illinois

Writtem by Debbie Dingerson, Lisa Cofield and Lea Rush

Cover Illustration by Design Dynamics, Glen Ellyn, IL

Published by Great Quotations Publishing Co.,
Glendale Heights, IL

ISBN 1-56245-222-3

Printed in Hong Kong

## Mrs. Murphy's Laws of Men

Mr. Murphy said if anything can go wrong, it will. (Mr. Murphy was a plumber.)

If at first you don't succeed, it's usually because your husband involved himself in the project.

The man who can't see dust on a table directly in front of him can see the swimsuit issue of Sports Illustrated from half a mile away.

If you spend three hours preparing a gourmet meal, he'll call to say he won't be home for dinner.

Women read Playgirl for the articles.

If you go to the grocery store wearing hair curlers and sweats, you'll run into the man of your dreams.

The night you try the "enhance your love life tip number three" by meeting him at the door in skimpy lingerie is the night he brings his parents home for dinner.

A man will spend forty-five minutes looking for the remote control to change to a half-hour program that ended fifteen minutes ago.

An apple a day keeps the doctor away, but if he's single and handsome, switch to oranges.

Four out of five single men think a formal dinner is anything that doesn't come in a Styrofoam container.

Once married, a man's door-opening gene goes dormant.

Husbands will go to any length to avoid taking the last square of toilet paper off the roll.

So will children.

The night you fix "left-over surprise" for dinner is the night he brings home his boss for dinner.

The VCR will conk out when your favorite movie and his "most important football game of the year" are on at the same time.

So will the spare television.

If anything can go wrong, it will ... in front
of the cute guy you are trying to impress.

No matter how closely you try to duplicate his mother's "secret recipe" for pumpkin pie, yours will never be as good.

His mother's "secret recipe" for pumpkin pie can usually be found on the back of the can.

Never date a man who drives a pick-up truck with silhouettes of well-endowed women on the mud flaps.

A man will usually ask if he can help right after you finish what you were doing.

As soon as you're working in the garden and covered with mud, your new boyfriend will stop by for a surprise visit.

If anything can go wrong, it will ... while your husband has the video camera rolling.

Five minutes after you call your boyfriend's answering machine and leave a message saying you never want to see him again, he'll call from his office and apologize because the fight was "all his fault."

The way to a man's heart is through his stomach.  The way to a woman's heart is through the doors of a restaurant.

Love is blind to everything except socks left on the floor.

When the going gets tough, the tough take a Diet Coke break.

Two's company and three's a crowd —
unless it's Sean Connery, chocolate and you.

It takes two to tango, but an unplanned pregnancy is all your fault.

Actions speak louder than words, so hold out for flowers whenever you can.

A watched phone never rings.

32

Never attempt a serious conversation with a
man during a playoff game.

*Correction:*
Never attempt any conversation with a man
during a playoff game.

Eight out of ten men believe they need a riding lawnmower to handle a 10′ by 10′ plot of grass.

## MRS. MURPHY'S LAWS
## OF DOMESTIC LIFE

If anything can go wrong, it will ... in front of your mother-in-law.

The day you forget your purse at home is the day a police officer will pull you over for a burned-out taillight.

The person you took off your Christmas
card list this year will send you one.

The length of the red light you are stopped at is directly proportional to how quickly you need to get where you are going.

If at first you don't succeed, turn it into a casserole.

Your car will stop making that "strange noise" once it's within earshot of the mechanic.

The volume of that "strange noise" is directly proportional to the cost of the repair.

The lettuce is always greener on the other side of the salad bar.

The first nice day after several rainy days is called "Monday".

One out of fifty shopping carts has a wobbly wheel, and you'll manage to find it every time.

Putting an item in a safe place guarantees you won't be able to find it when you need it.

(When you do find the item, it's usually three days after you needed it and are now looking for something else.)

Woman does not live by bread alone ... she needs chocolate fondue to dip it in.

If you drop a bag of groceries, it will be the one containing the eggs.

Regardless of which grocery line was moving fastest, it will become the slowest line once you stand in it.

The climactic end to a story line on your favorite soap will be pre-empted by a special news report of very little interest.

The most crucial ingredient in a recipe is the one you are out of.

The twenty-four hour flu rarely is.

Once you decide on the menu for your special gourmet dinner, you'll discover all the ingredients are out of season.

Birds of a feather flock together ... over your freshly-washed car.

Nine out of ten women are secretly hoping for the "Barbie with PMS" doll to hit the market. So is the tenth, but she was too busy eating chocolate chip cookies and potato chips to respond to the survey.

The really great photo that everyone wants
a copy of is the one you can't find the
negative for.

The more annoying the tune, the longer it takes to get it "out of your head".

The secluded tropical island you booked for your second honeymoon will have its first hurricane in 50 years the day after you arrive.

The one time you are late getting to the airport is the one time the plane leaves on time.

The length of the line at a public restroom is directly proportional to how badly you have to go.

Variety is the spice of life, but too much spice causes ulcers.

The longer you spend wrapping a present,
the faster it will be ripped apart by the
recipient.

People who live in glass houses have lots of windows to wash.

Three out of four summer weddings will be held outdoors on the hottest day of the year.  The fourth will be held indoors, but the air conditioning will be broken.

To make an omelette, you have to break a few eggs, chop the vegetables, grate the cheese, then clean up the mess afterward.

The Thanksgiving dinner that takes 20 hours to prepare will be completely devoured by your family in 20 minutes.

Rolling stones gather speed before they roll over your foot in the garden.

The amount of laundry soap in the bottom of the container is equal to one less than the number of loads of clothes you need to wash.

The one dish every member of your family raved about is the one you threw together on short notice and can't remember what you put in it.

A watched pot never boils.  An unwatched pot boils over, creating an awful mess on the stove.

Never let your husband pick out a
Christmas tree by himself.

Better late than never, unless you wanted to be pregnant.

The item you must have will be at the back
of the top shelf at the grocery store.

The German Shepherd you adopted to protect the house will hide under the bed at every strange noise it hears.

The grass growing in your driveway is always healthier than the grass in your yard.

The longest-lasting flower in your yard is usually the dandelion.

Your favorite television programs will all show at the same time on the same night.

What goes around comes around, and her name is "Mother-In-Law."

## MRS. MURPHY'S LAWS OF GENETICS

If anything can go wrong, it will .. with a carload full of children.

Nine out of ten children experience a sudden growth spurt the day after you purchase their back-to-school clothes.

Your son's revenge for being forced to take music lessons will be selecting the drums as his instrument of choice.

Junior will get hit in the mouth with a baseball the day after the braces are removed.

Children behave perfectly in public —
unless there are other people around.

Children only track mud on a "clean" floor.

Dogs do too.

The safest answer to a question beginning
"Mom, can I..." is always "no".

Children who can't get themselves out of bed on a school day will be up by 5 am to watch Saturday morning cartoons.

A bird in the hand is probably the pet your six-year-old promised to take care of, but hasn't noticed in three months.

No matter where you sit in a movie theater, you end up in front of a kid who's a seat-kicker.

The day after getting your daughter the kitten she's been begging for, you discover she's allergic to cats.

Taking the car any farther than the driveway causes children to say "I gotta go."

The day of school pictures, your kids will wear the weirdest outfits they can find.

If anything can go wrong, it will ... in front of the president of the PTA.

of the president of the PTA.

Don't put the shopping cart before a child who's been playing race car driver video games.

An optimist says a partial glass of grape juice is half full — a pessimist says it's half empty. Mrs. Murphy says either way, it will still be spilled on the new white carpet.

The "emergency" phone call from your six-year old will interrupt your staff meeting just as you've finished announcing a new policy limiting personal calls.

No news is good news, especially when it comes to hearing from the guidance counselor at your child's school.

Two heads are better than one, unless they belong to your teenager and his/her best friend.

The one night you get the kids to bed early
so you can watch your favorite TV show, it
will be a rerun.

(The rerun will be the one episode you actually
managed to see last year.)

There's no place like home, except a night in a hotel with no kids.

Where there's smoke, there's fire, and it's usually in the kitchen after your kids "surprise" you by cooking dinner.

Never leave the room just before the PTA is nominating someone to chair a committee.

The cheap vase is never the one that gets broken.

## MRS. MURPHY'S LAWS
## OF GLAMOUR

If anything can go wrong, it will ... as you're
getting dressed for your wedding.

If the shoe fits, it doesn't come in the color you need.

The nicer-looking the shoe, the more uncomfortable it is.

The blouse the dry-cleaner ruins will be your favorite one, and, of course, the most expensive.

When you find an eyeshadow color that looks fabulous on you, they discontinue it.

Most "theys" are men.

Beauty is only skin deep, but it takes three different types of moisturizer to make it happen.

If you need to stop at a red light to finish putting on your lipstick, all of the lights will be green.

All that glitters is not gold ... just make sure it's not cubic zirconia either.

If there's an outfit in your closet you haven't worn in a year, buy new shoes and jewelry to go with it.

A friend in need is a friend indeed. A friend who can eat anything she wants without gaining an ounce is no friend at all.

Wash and wear isn't.

Pre-shrunk jeans aren't either.

One size fits all doesn't.

When you've finally lost enough weight to fit into the clothes in the back of your closet, you discover they went out of style five years ago.

The shorter the skirt, the longer the run that starts at your thigh.

Shoulder pads make a fashion statement.
They say "linebacker".

Lightning never strikes twice in the same place. It just looks like it does every time you get a new perm.

Women with matching lipstick and nail polish have way too much time on their hands.

Sweaters that say "lay flat to dry" are usually 5" longer than the space you have to dry them in.

The squeaky wheel gets the grease all over your shoes, hands and slacks.

If you finally grow your nails long enough to have a manicure, you'll break two of them the day after you have it done.

The ugliness of the bridesmaid's dress your dear friend wants you to wear is directly proportional to how much you paid for it.

Your purse is never big enough to hold all the things you need to fit into it.

Neither is your closet.

Control top panty hose don't.

"All day comfort" bras and girdles aren't.

New and Improved isn't.

If 8 pairs of socks go into a dryer, 7.5 will come out.

When it rains, it pours ... then your new suede pumps get covered with mud.

If you find a gorgeous outfit on sale, the only jacket left will be one size too big and the only skirt will be one size too small.

Charity begins at home, so go buy yourself
that great-looking outfit.

Permanents aren't.

Thigh reducing cream doesn't.

Wrinkle hiding cream doesn't either.

Beauty is in the eye of the beholder ... and in the eye of your husband who thinks the skimpy lingerie he saw in a catalog would look "fabulous" on you.

Everyone tells you your hair looks great the day before you have an appointment to get it cut.

Inside every diet is a chocolate attack waiting to happen.

The worn-out tennis shoes with holes in them are always more comfortable than the ones you just bought.

## MRS. MURPHY'S LAWS
## OF BUSINESS

If anything can go wrong, it will ... in front
of your boss.

Your office Christmas party, his office Christmas party and your child's Christmas play will fall on the same evening.

A conversation that begins "this will only take a second" usually lasts two hours.

If you have a spare pair of panty hose in your desk, you won't run the ones you are wearing. If you don't have an extra pair, you will.

The amount of work piled on your desk is indirectly proportional to the amount of time you have to do it in.

The length of a traffic jam is directly proportional to how late you are for work.

If at first you don't succeed, find a convenient scapegoat.

The surest way to postpone a decision is to form a committee.

By the time you finally reach tech support for your computer, they've released a new version.

The day you're having your picture taken for the company newsletter is the day your face will break out.

The day after you work 20 hours revising a proposal, the client will go back to the original plan.

The person you just cut off in the parking lot will turn out to be the potential client you are meeting for the first time.

The day after you send out a memo reminding your staff they must be on time for work, you'll be late.

The crisis only you can solve will occur one day into a two-week vacation.

Mornings come much too early in the day.

The one phone call you've been waiting for all day will get forwarded to your voice mail because you answered a call from a long-distance service salesperson.

The length of time your boss spends talking at the morning staff meeting is directly proportional to how badly you want to take a nap.

Never put off until tomorrow what you can delegate today.

When opportunity knocks, run.

Bad news travels fast, but you're always the last to know.

## MRS. MURPHY'S LAWS
## OF ECONOMICS

If anything can go wrong it will ... and you can be sure the IRS will let you know about it.

"Free makeovers" at your favorite make-up counter usually end up costing at least $150.00.

If you have extra cash and go shopping,
you won't find anything you like.

A fool and his money are usually protected by a pre-nuptial agreement.

Math errors made while balancing the checkbook almost always result in a lower balance.

The ugly vase you sold at a garage sale for $3 will turn out to be a collector's item worth $200.

A warranty will usually cover everything except the part that needs to be replaced.

(The part that needs to be replaced is the one part that will take three weeks to get because it needs to be ordered.)

A penny saved collects interest on which you have to pay taxes, so you might as well go shopping instead.

Buying new towels leads to the need to redecorate the entire master bathroom, which in turn leads to the need to redecorate the entire bedroom.

People who have their Christmas shopping done before the Fourth of July have way too much time on their hands.

There's strength in numbers, especially those to the left of the decimal point.

The best things in life are free ... NOT!

Tomorrow is another day, unless you win the lottery.

Better late than never. Of course, you'll have to pay the interest and penalties on what you still owe to the IRS.

Absence makes the heart grow fonder and the phone bills grow larger.

Immediately after an expensive home repair, a co-worker will tell you she knows someone who could have done it for half the cost.

Convenience stores aren't.

Discount stores are, but there's usually a good reason for that.

# OTHER TITLES BY GREAT QUOTATIONS

199 Useful Things to Do With A Politician
201 Best Things Ever Said
A Lifetime of Love
A Light Heart Lives Long
A Teacher Is Better Than Two Books
As A Cat Thinketh
Cheatnotes On Life
Chicken Soup
Dear Mr. President
Don't Deliberate . . . Litigate
Father Knows Best
Food For Thought
For Mother–A Bouquet of Sentiments
Golden Years, Golden Words
Happiness Walks On Busy Feet
Heal The World
Hooked on Golf
Hollywords
I'm Not Over The Hill
In Celebration of Women
Interior Design For Idiots
Life's Simple Pleasures

Money For Nothing, Tips For Free
Motivation Magic
Mrs. Murphy's Laws
Mrs. Webster's Dictionary
Mrs. Webster's Guide To Business
Parenting 101
Real Estate Agents and Their
   Dirty Little Tricks
Reflections
Romantic Rendezvous
The Sports Page
So Many Ways To Say Thank You
Some Things Never Change
The ABC's of Parenting
The Best of Friends
The Birthday Astrologer
The Little Book of Spiritual Wisdom
The Secret Language of Men
The Secret Language of Women
Things You'll Learn, If You Live
   Long Enough
Women On Men

**GREAT QUOTATIONS PUBLISHING COMPANY**
1967 Quincy Court
Glendale Heights, IL 60139-2045
Phone (708) 582-2800
Fax (708) 582-2813